Songs for a Mechanical Age

A Collection of Steampunk Poetry

By Stephen Sanders

Blackbead Books
2013

To Captain Jane Jasper & the Right Reverend Dr. Scott:
without the two of you this would never have happened!

Songs for a Mechanical Age Copyright ©2013 by
Stephen Sanders

ISBN: 978-0615805399

An Introduction

"Steampunk" has been a recognized sub-genre of science fiction and fantasy since, at least, the late nineteen-eighties. But there are examples of this type of literature going all the way back to the works of Jules Verne, H.G. Wells, and Edgar Rice Burroughs. Broadly defined, "steampunk" refers to a thematic universe that features steam-powered technology and a Victorian-era setting. Put another way, it is an alternate history, fantasy world where steam has remained the primary source of power. However one defines this hybrid genre, Steampunk is a wonderful place to play.

In addition to all of the books and stories and films and creative people who are involved in this revolution, there are conventions and festivals which feature, either exclusively or as a large part, Steampunk fashions, props, quasi-inventions, and the genre as a general attitude. There are Steampunk toys for sale in shops. There are Steampunk clothes that one can purchase from the Internet or in shops or at festivals. Even popular television has embraced Steampunk. In short, there is an entire subculture devoted to Steampunk that exists today.

So, why not Steampunk poetry? Not just poetry that includes the basic themes of the genre but an actual poetic form or body of work that is identified as "Steampunk poetry." Just as so many modern or antique objects have been modded by individuals into a pseudo-Victorian style, why not take an existing form and mold it into a unique stylistic expression of this sub-genre? Why not, indeed!

There are many, many Victorian era poets and poetry forms to draw from in this literary odyssey. But one form seems to fit the bill perfectly: the triolet. The triolet is an antique form which has an almost mechanical set of format requirements but has enough flexibility to allow for a human touch.

Traditionally, the triolet is a stanza poem of eight lines. Its rhyme scheme is *ABaAabAB* and often, but not always, all lines are in iambic tetrameter. The first, fourth and seventh lines are identical, as are the second and final lines, thereby making the initial and final couplets identical as well. Another variation often seen in the triolet is that the lines which are supposed to be identical can be slightly varied if the imaginative change is clever enough.

The triolet was developed in the late thirteenth century as a French form but has enjoyed a number of periods of popularity. Most notably, the triolet was re-popularized by the renowned Victorian era poet, Thomas Hardy. The almost mathematical rules, the period of popularity during the Victorian Era, and the flexibility to allow a vivid imagination to take flight – all of these elements seem to make the triolet the perfect poem for the Steampunk genre.

So saying, we invite you to enjoy these pieces and let them transport you to this dreamed-of era: half voyage of fantasy, half historical adventure, with a liberal application of technology, and resulting in a great deal of fun! Steampunk is going to be around forever and now it even has its own poetry!

YESTERDAY, TODAY, TOMORROW and SEVERAL SIDEWISE PERSPECTIVES ON A PACK OF LIES

Forewards Backwards Sidewards
An Essay From The Right Reverend Dr Scott

Those who do not remember the past are condemned to repeat it.
George Santayana

I like the dreams of the future better than the history of the past.
Thomas Jefferson

History is a gallery of pictures in which there are few originals and many copies.
Alexis de Tocqueville

History is the version of past events that people have decided to agree upon.
Napoleon Bonaparte

History is a pack of lies about events that never happened told by people who weren't there.
George Santayana

What is history? I don't know: I wasn't there.

Were you there? Did you write it all down? Did you tell the truth?

What is truth?

So far, all I got is "history is a bunch of made up answers for a bunch of made up questions about what might or might not have happened."

"OR NOT."

If we are gonna argue all day over "What is history?" we are never gonna agree on "What is Steampunk?" Cause it seems like no two Steamy Punks can ever agree on exactly what Steampunk is or is not.

And we got 1001 different opinions on "what is history?" coming from 1001 allegedly famous guys named Abraham, Winston, Napoleon, Jefferson, de Toqueville and Santayana (loved his first three albums, then he got all Haha-vishnu for a while and I lost him)

"I don't know Alexis de Toqueville but I know what I like". Yeah I like the retro future and I like the retro futuristic visonary triolets of Stephen Sanders, who I know best as "Blackbead the Pirate Laureate", here reinvented as a complete A.S.S. (air steam ship) Commander.

Looking ahead backwards into your future, as you read this book of verse, Steve Sanders writes in his triolet "The New Century":

"We are poised on the brink of a brand new age:
The Mechanical Revolution is about to start!"

We bring to the reading our pre conditioned notions of "The Industrial Revolution" as we sort of half assed learned it in long lost long ago "history classes" we were all forced to sleepwalk through in those far away "school days". We can infer that Steve Sanders is playing with our perceptions of those concepts.

He continues:

"What sort of play will we enact on this stage
We are poised to enter? A whole new age
Will be written, page by glorious page!"

I find double or even triple meanings here. The uncommunicated, unspoken but almost agreed upon conceptions of a Steampunk Aesthetic allow us to reflect upon what happened, what might have happened, what should have happened, an aesthetic that allows both writer and reader to re-suppose past, present, future, yesterday, today and tomorrow, and rewrite history with no pre-agreed upon notions of what "history" might actually be.

This particular piece, which I consider to be the heart of this overall work, concludes:

"A whole new science; unimaginable art!"

This could reflect on back to the ideas of "what the hell is history anyway?" and "what the hell is this "Steampunk" thing?" It is science, it is art, it is defined somewhere between the writer and the reader, and somewhere in there is a closer answer to these basic silly questions that frame the mechanical heart and artificial soul of my thesis and foreword to this book.

Finally, in the convention of the triolet, Sanders repeats his first couplet:

"We are poised on the brink of a brand new age:
The Mechanical Revolution is about to start!"

His verse is poised on the brink of the past as it looks ahead in a mechanical way that tells of human spirit while rewriting and retelling the stories of humankind.

Or not.

For perhaps that is what "history" is: the telling of our stories of humankind.

OR NOT.

I wasn't there, I didn't know the famous guys, I have heard the stories, so the "lessons" of history are the human values and ideas we pass along and share.

Why not have alternative history told as "Steampunk"? How do we know that "history" isn't some kind of alternative universe to begin with?

You won't find any answers in my essay: you may or may not find many answers in Stephen Sanders' book of verse. But you may find momentary amusement and some room for the provocation of your thoughts. And that is a very good justification for the existence of poetry.

Take that, now go write your own alternative tales of past, present and future.

~The Right Reverend Doctor Scott
2013

Table of Contents

Triolets

Other Poems

Triolets

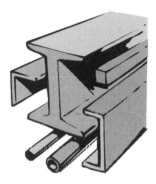

The Metal Age

Brass, bronze, copper and steel,
Building blocks for our modern age.
Things with substance; things that are real:
Brass, bronze, copper, and steel.
Warm to the touch but it's the steam you feel;
We take our power from the boiling rage.
Bronze, copper, brass and steel,
Building blocks for our mechanical age.

Steampunk Nation

Tinkerers, tailors, crafters, and mages:
The people of the Steampunk 'verse.
With cogs and brass we earn our wages,
We tinkerers, tailors, crafters, and mages.
But in dreams, we emerge from the written pages
Of novels and graphic tales diverse.
Tinkerers, tailors, crafters, and mages:
The people of the Steampunk 'verse.

Goliath

Amazing power, how she can soar!
My airship, *Goliath*, takes flight!
Hear those engines? Listen to that roar!
Amazing power! How she can soar
Allows me to conquer and explore
All the lands within my sight!
Amazing power, how I can soar!
My airship, *Goliath*, takes flight!

The Last Stand

As the sun sinks slowly in the west,
Our day is almost done.
We fall in place as if seeking rest
As the sun sinks slowly. In the west,
The enemy presses; will we survive this test?
We will win to glory or we will die as one.
As the sun sinks slowly in the west,
Our day is almost done.

Into the Night

Follow me, into the night,
And I'll take you where you want to go.
Pull down your hat and douse that light;
Follow me. Into the night,
We'll let our souls take flight
And learn what others dare not know.
Follow me, into the night,
And I'll take you where you want to go.

Into the Night
(A Variation)

Follow me, into the night,
And I'll take you where the dead men go.
Screw up your courage but douse that light;
Follow me. Into the night,
We'll let our nightmares take flight
And walk where the reaper's minions sow.
Follow me, into the night,
And I'll take you where the dead men go.

The Strand

As I stand here with my face to the sea,
The wind and a memory caress my skin.
Thoughts of you rush back to me
As I stand here with my face to the sea.
There is no where else I would rather be
For on this strand you live again.
As I stand here with my face to the sea,
The wind, and a memory, caresses my skin.

The Nautilus

Slipping through the darkest depths of the sea,
A metal avenger shines through the gloom.
Your master's heart must pay the fee,
Slipping through the darkest depths of the sea,
Losing life's warmth degree by degree...
But then you rise to show the world its doom!
Slipping through the darkest depths of the sea,
A metal avenger shines through the gloom.

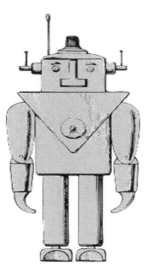

Man of Steam

From two opposing elements you are born;
Water and fire are your blood and soul.
Hissing alive on a cold, gray morn,
From two opposing elements you are born:
Gallons of clear water you guzzle from a horn
But your heart ignites with the blackest coal!
From two opposing elements you are born;
Water and fire are your blood and soul.

The New Century

We are poised on the brink of a brand new age:
The Mechanical Revolution is about to start!
What sort of play will we enact on this stage
We are poised to enter? A whole new age
Will be written, page by glorious page!
A whole new science; unimaginable art!
We are poised on the brink of a brand new age:
The Mechanical Revolution is about to start!

Steam Attacker*

Out of the cold, gray mists I rise
In my Attacker to face the foe.
The sun behind me, I dive in surprise
Into the cold, gray mists. I rise
Again before my enemy's eyes,
Their machines burning brightly below!
Out of the cold, gray mists I rise
In my Attacker to face the foe.

*A "steam attacker" is a type of flying machine from an alternate universe I
developed for a series of short stories which, hopefully, will become a novel
someday. It is based on technology successfully developed in 1933 by George
D. and William J. Bessler. Steam-powered aircraft have been built and flown
successfully several times in history. The "Bessler Arabian" is a steam-
powered biplane developed in my alternate universe following the initial
failure of the Martian attack on the Earth in H.G. Well's War of the Worlds.
The short stories are based on the premise that not all of the Martians were
killed in the plague that followed their arrival on Earth and that mankind,
stealing some of the Martian technology, has begun a war to drive the
remnants of the invaders from their planet. The "Arabian" is a biplane which
features a steam engine using an alien power source, giving it much more
successful, and useful, aerodynamic capabilities; early twentieth century
weaponry; and "reflective armor" to reduce the effects of the Martian death
ray.

The Dark Continent

Deepest, darkest Africa! We search your lands
In vain for gold, diamonds and lore.
We find a thousand ways to die at your hands,
Deepest, darkest Africa. We search your lands
And find lions, disease, and fast-flowing sands;
Thirsty shadows surround us by the score.
Deepest, darkest Africa; we search your lands,
Insane, for gold, diamonds and lore.

The Vapor Phase

I remember when you were like water, flowing,
And we were the fire in your heart.
Remember how the pressure was always growing?
I remember. When you were like water, flowing,
And our love, like coals, was red-hot glowing!
Oh! Remember how we were at the start?
I remember when you were like water, flowing,
And we were the fire in your heart.

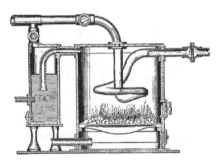

Manila Bay

Dewey and his greyhounds crept into Manila Bay.
Their pace relentless and steady
As they neared the break of day.
Dewey and his greyhounds crept into Manila Bay,
Thinking of the Maine, the Commodore was heard to say:
"Gridley, you may fire when ready."
Dewey and his greyhounds leapt into Manila Bay,
Their salvos relentless and steady.

The Stream of Time

One day I shall call upon many ancient races,
Visiting them as I travel through time.
I cannot wait to see their worlds, their faces,
One day. I shall call upon many ancient races
Confident that the wheel of the multiverse erases
Any paradox in Earth's reason or rhyme.
One day I shall call upon many ancient races,
Visiting them as I travel through time.

Time Untamed

Time, such an elusive and feral steed,
Is a bronc we all seek to master.
Many try to avoid age but all must heed
Time. Such an elusive and feral steed,
And to break it, from all that I read,
Is a feat that would invite disaster.
Time, such an elusive and feral steed,
Is a bronc we all seek to master.

Tangram

Cogs and spindles, rods and wheels,
Puzzle pieces with no definite solution.
Like cards, the engineer shuffles and deals
Cogs and spindles, rods and wheels.
Their limitless usage, at last, reveals
The shape of our mechanical revolution.
Cogs and spindles, rods and wheels,
Puzzle pieces with an infinite solution.

The Summer of 1899

They came at us, from the void of space,
Intent on destroying our dream.
Like the Mongols of old, a warrior race,
They came at us. From the void of space
They find themselves face to face
With our steel and our boiling steam.
They came at us across the void of space...
It is we who are destroying their dream.

Meandering Serenity

Gliding serenely, down a meandering creek,
My steam-powered canoe and I,
The company of nature is what we seek,
Gliding serenely down a meandering creek,
Propelled by paddles made of the finest teak,
The mechanical arms make nary a squeak
As we pass 'neath the trees and the sky.
Gliding serenely, down a meandering creek
My steam-powered canoe and I.

The Miners

Working below you, down in the pits,
We are the miners who dig your coal.
Sweating in darkness, scared out of our wits,
Working below you. Down in the pits
When the light and the good air quits...
Dear God, please save my soul!
Working below you, down in the pits,
We are the miners who dig your coal.

Walking Near Aschensegne Tor

Let me find a way to unpeel the years
So I can send my senses reeling
To Hardy's birds and Tennyson's spears!
Let me find a way!   To unpeel the years,
I must only invent a machine that steers
Me to an overflow of powerful feeling.
Oh, let me find a way to unpeel the years
So I can send my senses reeling!

In the Steamhouse

Bright yellow and burning red,
See my steamhouse flowers grow!
The steam turns the daffodil bed
Bright yellow burning! A red
Anthurium raises a glossy head!
The mist makes the cautleyas glow
Bright yellow and burning red!
Oh, see my steamhouse flowers grow!

I Found Myself at a Crystal Cave

I found myself at a crystal cave;
There I boldly entered.
Between a hero and a knave,
I found myself.   At a crystal cave,
Listening to a mad priest rave,
My soul was shriven, then centered.
I found myself at a crystal cave:
There, I boldly entered.

Such a Lovely ASS* *Beulah!*

Ahoy! Here she flies! A shapely airship
Making way under a full head of steam!
She seems to be coming at a rather brisk clip!
Ahoy! Here she comes! A shapely airship
With a full treasure chest and a firm helm to grip
Is every lusty airship pirate's dream!
Ahoy! How she flies! A shapely airship
Making way under a full head of steam!

*"ASS" is the international designation for "Air Steam Ship"

Honor's Courage

"First will come the draw, then will come the lightning,
And after, only one of you still standing."
(breathing ragged, knuckles whitening…)
"First will come the draw, then will come the lightning…"
(sweat running free, stomach muscles tightening…)
Honor cannot ease the course she is demanding.
"First will come the draw, then will come the lightning,
And after, only one of you still standing."

Other Poems

Land Leviathan

I push the Johnson bar forward
And open the cylinder cocks,
Steam slips through copper pipes
And my leviathan steps away from the docks.

I open the throttle completely
And raise the thing's battering arm;
My plan is to crush the enemy
Before they can raise the alarm.

I look down from my battle station,
Fully ten meters in the air,
I can see their cavalry running,
I can sense their panic and despair.

As I trod on their fixed positions
And kick their guns to and fro,
An officer stops in his frenzy
And shoots his pistol at me from below.

Bouncing off three inches of armor
His bullets do very little harm;
I turn to my puny opponent
And lower the great battering arm.

I point at him with a huge finger,
I know my position is supreme,
Through a pipe running down into the digit
I could roast him alive with pure steam!

He finally drops his weapon and,
Turning, runs from the field
With six leviathans in action,
The enemy combatants swiftly yield.

This battlefield sinks into silence
But will this war we fight ever cease?
I wonder if my great land leviathan
Will ever walk this Earth in peace?

For now, my machine needs tending,
So I re-open the cylinder cocks,
The steam refills the same copper tubes
And my giant turns back to the docks.

"Mistery" Woman

Black leather and black lace,
you glide into the room like steam,
hot, "misterious," and full of power.

Raising your goggles,
your sapphire eyes scan the room,
seeking out your precision, transition fit partner.

As the orchestra begins a waltz,
you glide along in your own dance:
a smile, a look, a tilt of your head;
leaving the men in your wake wondering
wishing, yet afraid to follow you.

But you are fearless, confident, secure
in the knowledge that you will either
find the one you seek
or simply vanish back into the night,
back to one of the other countless pursuits
that tickle your fancy.

Like your glass, you fill every day,
every night, to the fullest.
But some nights are for burgundy,
some nights are for whiskey,
and some nights are for fresh, clear water.
What will you drink your fill of tonight?

Black leather and black lace,
you glide through the room like steam,
hot, "misterious," and full of power.

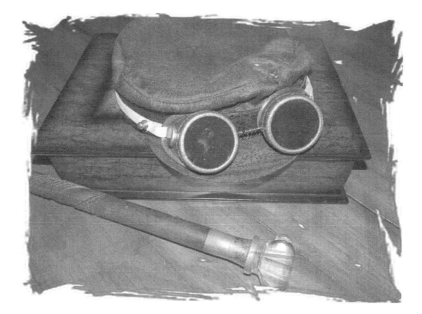

Blow, Bugle, Blow

The splendour falls on castle walls
And snowy summits old in story:
The long light shakes across the lakes,
And the wild cataract leaps in glory.
Blow, bugle, blow, set the wild echoes flying,
Blow, bugle; answer, echoes, dying, dying, dying.

O hark, O hear! how thin and clear,
And thinner, clearer, farther going!
O sweet and far from cliff and scar
The horns of Elfland faintly blowing!
Blow, let us hear the purple glens replying:
Blow, bugle; answer, echoes, dying, dying, dying.

O love, they die in yon rich sky,
They faint on hill or field or river:
Our echoes roll from soul to soul,
And grow for ever and for ever.
Blow, bugle, blow, set the wild echoes flying,
And answer, echoes, answer, dying, dying, dying.

Alfred, Lord Tennyson

Blow, Whistle, Blow

A response, grounded in hope,
to our great Laureate's "Blow, Bugles, Blow!"

The stoker wipes wet off the pipes
And shovels coal amid the flames.
The red light leaps across the heaps
As steam the modern engine tames.
Blow, whistle, blow, proclaim the future coming!
Blow, whistle; answer, pistons, drumming, drumming, drumming!

O, hark, O hear! How loud and clear,
And stronger as it nears!
The sound of progress bringing cheer:
The rhythmic chatter of the gears!
Blow, steam trumpet echoes humming
Blow, whistle; answer, pistons, drumming, drumming, drumming!

On, Science! You advance sans abeyance
All Man's ills to alleviate;
Healing all disease, filling life with ease,
What can our minds not create?
Blow, whistle, blow, announce the future coming!
Blow, whistle; answer, pistons, drumming, drumming, drumming!

If you enjoyed these works, you might be interested in some of the other books offered by Blackbead Books –

Raising Black Flags: Poetry about pirates by people who KNOW the pirate life! Read "A Tale From Devil's Tavern"! "The Last Watch"! "So You Want to Be a Pirate?" "Dark Prince of Plunder"! "The Old Sea Captain"! And dozens of other great pirate poems from fourteen different poets!

Echoes From Other Worlds: Poetry and short stories, half are pirate-themed and half are science fiction/fantasy. "Treasured Melody", "Vagabond", "Legend of the Compass Rose", "The Portal", "The Mayan Project", and so many more!

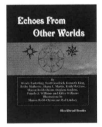

A Nest of Pirates, Characters, and so many more! Go to our website – www.blackbead-jewelry.com – or put "stephen sanders poetry" into any search engine and you'll find us!